PENGUIN BOOKS

CATTITUDES

Elizabeth King Brownd is widely known for her richly detailed and unique cat portraits. Her work appears on fine art prints and decorative gifts throughout the world. She has illustrated numerous books; however, this book represents her first published writing.

Elizabeth lives with her husband, their three children, four horses, two dogs and twelve cats on a farm in Mossyrock, Washington.

◆ ◆ ❖ ◆ ◆

CATTITUDES

From A

_To_ Z

ELIZABETH KING BROWND

PENGUIN BOOKS

PENGUIN BOOKS

Published by the Penguin Group
Penguin Putnam Inc., 375 Hudson Street, New York, New York 10014, USA
Penguin Books Ltd, 27 Wrights Lane, London W8 5TZ
Penguin Books Australia Ltd, Ringwood, Victoria, Australia
Penguin Books Canada Ltd, 10 Alcorn Avenue, Toronto, Ontario, Canada M4V 3B2
Penguin Books (NZ) Ltd, 182-190 Wairau Road, Auckland 10, New Zealand

Penguin Books Ltd, Registered Offices: Harmondsworth, Middlesex, England

First published in the United Kingdom by Michael Joseph Ltd. 1997
Published in Penguin Books (USA) 1998
3 5 7 9 10 8 6 4 2

ISBN 0 14 026874 X

Printed in Italy

**For my mother and father,
Mary and Gordon**

Special thanks to Mark
for his skill and tenacity
and to his unwavering partiality
for pure white cats

And many thanks to my girls,
Teletha, Samantha and Jennifer

Our Feline Frenzy

♦♦❖♦♦

Several years ago, we realized that we were among the chosen. Our entire family had been irrevocably lured into voluntary servitude. Our cats had come to claim us. Perhaps it was predestined. We would have never dreamed that one day we would join the ranks of devoted cat lovers. Why was this event so inconceivable to us? The truth, I must confess, is that we were die-hard dog lovers.

If you have not already slammed this book shut, I will, in the next pages, attempt to redeem myself.

It all began with our only pet, a dog named Gus. His beguiling nature captured our hearts but, unfortunately, he had destructive habits. Daily there were new surprises, ripped up flower beds or missing tennis shoes,

but one day his antics became, shall we say, utterly shocking. While I was vacuuming, he chewed through the electrical cord. Luckily, he recovered, although was always a bit daffy.

It was at this point that we became weary of his never-ending shenanigans. We decided that perhaps what he needed was animal companionship, a playmate (or two) to keep him occupied. And so, over the next few years, our menagerie grew – we acquired four horses, two cows, and two more dogs. We soon realized we had more than we could manage and vowed to resist the temptation to acquire any new animals.

One fateful day, however, my two small boys returned from a visit to the home of nearby friends. They were glee-fully clutching a small box, a present from our friends. My husband, Richard, and I watched them as they excitedly opened the box. How lovely, we thought, expecting some home-made sweets or a cake perhaps?

To our dismay, in the very bottom of the box sat a chubby little mouse! Of course, the children begged to be allowed to keep it. Richard would have none of it. 'Absolutely *NOT*!' he roared. He spent the rest of the afternoon grumbling on about the mouse, vengefully consider-ing an appropriate gift to bestow upon our 'friends' who had so kindly given us a rodent.

Assorted Biscuits

Tearfully, the children continued to plead with their father to let them keep the mouse. Patiently, he explained that mice were vile, vandalous and unsanitary creatures. But to the children, this small creature was bright eyed, sweet and perfectly loveable. Above all, how could their father be so heartless to turn out a homeless mouse?

By bedtime, however, the boys had worn him down with promises that the mouse would always be kept in its box and be no trouble – and so the mouse, which the children named Hyper, was allowed to stay.

Several nights later, during a fit of insomnia, our pudgy mouse gnawed a hole in the box and managed to squeeze out.

In a few weeks' time, the reason for Hyper's rotundity became apparent. We were overrun with mice. When Richard discovered the mice had made a nest in his ski boot, he threw a fit. Spitefully, he assumed the dismal task of setting mouse traps where the kids wouldn't discover them because there was no way of knowing which mouse was Hyper. After a few weeks, however, the traps proved to be ineffective.

Every night, Richard faithfully set the 'foolproof' contraptions with cheese, and by morning the little varmints had cleverly sprung the traps and scurried away unharmed, taking the cheese with them. Obviously, Hyper's offspring were more ingenious than we had imagined. The mouse dilemma brought us face to face with the inevitable.

We needed a cat.

We heard about one that had been caught in a rabbit snare and was in need of a home. It turned out to be cantankerous and decidedly unsociable. No one seemed overly distraught when it ran away two weeks later. We foolishly wondered if perhaps the mice would follow suit. No such luck. It was my mother who, in her infinite wisdom, offered advice: 'What you need is a pregnant cat. That way, when she has kittens, she will stay.' Stupendous idea, we thought.

With the local animal shelter having an unprecedented shortage of cats, I began to wonder how on earth I would find a pregnant cat. After making several inquiries, no one could recall seeing any stray cats about, let alone a cat with the qualification of being conspicuously pregnant. We displayed a notice in a nearby shop, which solicited one reply. The caller desperately needed a home for his cat, named Princess.

According to his description, she was the ideal house cat, a young, fetching, long-haired puss with procreative potential. We drove into town with the boys to have a look at her. After a few minutes, my husband ascertained that Princess was not, in fact, a Princess but a Prince! We also guessed that his age was perhaps under-estimated by at least ten years. We declined as politely as possible and wished the owner luck in finding the Prince a new home.

What I am about to tell you next is as believable as the moon being made of green cheese. It is, however, the absolute truth. A fortnight passed and we were still lamenting our kittylessness. One evening, my husband was coming home from work and arrived at the front gate only to discover not one, but two stray cats, both obviously pregnant. One was black and the other white. Word had obviously got out on the feline grapevine that a good home was in the offing.

Richard walked in the door, announcing the arrival of allied forces with concealed troops of demousers. He referred to them as Her Majesty and Snagglepuss. However, the boys affectionately called our expectant mothers Mumsy and Tumsy – and Mumsy and Tumsy they remained. We made them two snug little beds inside cardboard boxes and a few weeks later, we had twelve kittens. No two were alike, a delightfully mismatched medley. They were all so precious. We were completely transfixed and the boys were in seventh heaven.

Within weeks the kittens had ventured out of the kitty basket and were everywhere, in any drawer and cupboard left open, under foot or climbing up the curtains. One morning, we found a kitten snugly curled up on top of my freshly baked banana bread, the warmest place in the house.

As the cats became more active, we realized we were living in a feline Jurassic Park. You often hear about those rather eccentric people who live with zillions of cats. We started wondering if we were becoming a bit peculiar ourselves.

One evening Richard announced that he had done some mathematical calculations regarding our cat population. 'Do you know,' he said, 'we could have as many as sixty cats in a year's time, and in two years' time ...' We had to do something. It was then that we made our first sane decision. We took the young cats to our local veterinary surgeon to have them rendered, er ... 'unreproduceable'. Imagine how happy our vet was when, upon our arrival, he acquired twelve new surgical admissions. Imagine how unhappy we were when we received the bill. Although not quite our life savings, we could nevertheless have replaced all the clawed furniture and shredded curtains. I winced, thinking how I could have bought a whole new wardrobe minus the cat hairs.

Richard and I tossed around a few ideas to help defray expenses. Raise fancy purebreds and sell them? Rent them out by the afternoon to elderly ladies in need of companionship? Take them to Chinatown?

Being an illustrator, I began painting cats doing silly things. After all, I had no shortage of live models. Eventually, I had several paintings for which I wrote accompanying verse. So here is the whole kit and caboodle, all of my paintings over three years, minus two pictures. The one Ms. Kitty mistook for a scratching post and the other baby Cocoa christened. This last one dried and appears to be in good condition but I didn't have the guts to send it to Jenny Dereham, my editor.

Cats are Amiable

• • ❖ • •

The most charming creatures under the sun are cats. Fully aware of their irresistible nature, cats can afford to be selective in their choice of companions. They have a knack of becoming chummy with humans of a subservient nature. In the absence of such a person, cats prefer the companionship of other cats who are models of feline perfection.

Cats are Beguiling

••❖••

Most people acquire their first cat quite unintentionally. One fateful look into the eyes of a cat and your life will be changed forever. You will be completely spellbound when they slip through your door, finding new territory for their claws and cat hairs. Cheer up. Your house may soon be in a shambles, but you'll always have your little darling.

Cats are Cryptic

••❖••

Cats lead mysterious lives. They can disappear for days at a time. The little vagabonds are struck with routine wanderlust and never reveal their whereabouts. Perhaps there are secret feline havens where cats leading double lives take refuge.

D

Cats are Dignified

✦

Felines can often be observed in solitary contemplation. Aloofness in cats is reflected in their superior composure. Unlike dogs, cats are reserved. A cat, for instance, would never be found howling at the moon.

Cats are Egotistical

••❖••

Don't get overly excited when you discover your cat reading this book. Your little pet is not attempting to share your literary interest so that the two of you can engage in intelligent conversation. Your cat is studying the pictures so he can come up with a clever pose and make an appearance on the next book's cover.

Cats are Finicky

· · ❖ · ·

Cats instinctively prefer gourmet foods. Contrary to popular opinion, they do not like to eat rodents or raw, unplucked canaries. Keeping up with Kitty's special treats, like fresh roast chicken and fish fleurettes, is not always convenient. When you're serving cold leftover stew and Kitty gives you an evil stare, remind him that in some parts of the world he would be considered an ingredient.

Cats are Gracious

❖

The well-bred cat is respectful of all members of catkind however diverse their ancestral lineage may be. The well-mannered cat extends open-hearted kindness even to cats of unusual or dubious descent. The fellowship of cats is noted for its solidarity.

Cats are Hygienic

• • ❖ • •

Cats abhor dirt, filth or foul matter of any kind. Excessive shedding and kitty dandruff can be quite embarrassing. Cleanliness means daily grooming rituals. Fluffy tails and peticurred paws are a sign of a clean kitty. Full-submersion bathing for cats shows promise but is still in its experimental stages.

I

Cats are Inebriate

• • ❖ • •

Occasionally, your cat may appear deranged. Before your cat reaches its second birthday, it would be wise to have a little chat concerning substance abuse. These days, old-fashioned cat-mint or catnip tea may have additives. If, upon observation, your cat appears to be unusually daffy, you may safely assume that the cat is indeed blotto.

J

Cats are Jealous

❖

If your household has more than one cat, be certain to divide your affections equally. You may think that everything is going fine, but they are keeping score. Two pats for Jules and two pats for Jim. When Jules gets a new toy and Jim doesn't, take cover. Screaming cat fights are totally unnerving. When the fur flies, stand back. If one cat starts to resemble mincemeat, it's time for a bucket of water.

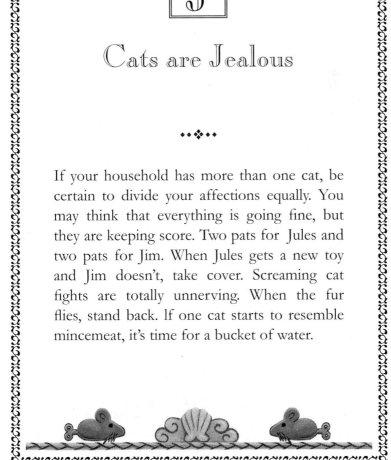

Cats are Kleptomaniacal

• • ❖ • •

Searching for missing items of a personal nature can be irritating. Do you ever wonder if you have resident poltergeists in your house? Namely, your cats. While you're busy at the office, they're busy re-arranging your drawers. Count your lucky stars if you never come home unexpectedly and discover your tom cat wearing your lingerie.

Cats are Lucky

••❖••

Don't be fooled by the 'poor wittle kitty' routine. Not only do cats have nine lives so they can live longer, but thousands of little old ladies leave entire estates to cats who then live better than you do. Looking to feather your own nest? First, find your little old lady, then introduce her to your irresistible cat.

Cats are Mischievous

⋄

Or, more like, devious. Cats are the masters of intrigue and strategy. Game playing begins at an early age. Two traditional games that every kitten knows are Hide and Seek (useful when it is time to go to the vet) and Bag the Birdie (just for fun or between-meal snacks).

Cats are Nonproductive

••❖••

Notwithstanding their ability to produce scores of kittens, cats actually do very little. These quintessential lounge lizards tend to suffer from chronic inertia, snoozing as many as twenty hours a day. The four remaining hours are spent (1) eating, (2) staring into space, (3) visiting the goldfish, and (4) contemplating the next nap.

Cats are Observant

•• ❖ ••

Among cats the art of espionage is highly val-
ued. Bird watching is ideal for developing skills
in observation which can be later used to detect
any suspicious goings on among humans. We
do not want high-tech spy devices to get into
the wrong paws, however; the world has
enough Peeping Toms.

Cats are Presumptuous

••❖••

After acquiring their first cat, most people are thoroughly amazed by the speed and agility with which a singular cat can take over the entire household. Don't forget house cats are the descendants of the great cats who ruled the jungles. For a moment, assume that one half of the people in the world has cats, then multiply that number by six. Then Chairman Meow steps in and gives the word 'catastrophe' a whole new meaning.

Cats are Quirky

••❖••

Humans rudely refer to cats as destructive animals, especially when the new house plants appear clawed or chewed. Nothing could be further from the truth. If left alone, the clever cat will develop unusual talents to the pinnacle of artistic expression. Your rose bushes and shrubs provide excellent pruning material for the feline horticultural novice.

Cats are Refined

••❖••

Cats have a well-developed appreciation for the arts. Art historians remark that many of Leonardo's notebooks contain exquisite drawings of cats. Although none of the master's oil paintings depicting cats has ever been catalogued, several are believed to be held in private collections. Cats with artistic savvy can spot a priceless masterpiece anywhere.

S

Cats are Sophisticated

Compared to humans, cats have more highly refined auditory and sensory perception. Imagine how thrilling it will be when box office managers show proper decorum and finally permit felines to attend their greatest musical tribute, *Cats*.

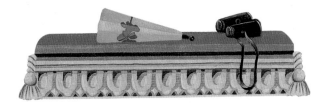

Cats are Telepathic

❖

In the animal kingdom, cats are recognized universally for their intuitive nature. They are instinctively aware of impending danger round every corner. Felines, as a species, have survived millenniums due to their highly developed ESP. The nine-lives theory was probably a gross under-estimation made by some dimwit who observed cats but died before his cats did.

Cats are Useless

•• ❖ ••

Sad, but true. Consider the following comparative study.

Animal Occupations	Dogs	Cats
Guarding humans	Yes	No
Leading the blind	Yes	No
Mountain rescue	Yes	No
Fire rescue	Yes	No
Assisting the police	Yes	No
Herding livestock	Yes	No

(Cats prefer the indulgent life, dabbling in useless pastimes which require a minimum of physical exertion.)

Cats are Vain

••❖••

Vanity in cats is part of their allure. They are naturally seductive when it comes to playing the role of Glamourpuss. It is an indisputable fact that cats are exquisitely beautiful creatures, and they simply know it.

Cats are Well Groomed

••❖••

The fashionable cat always keeps up appearances and wears the appropriate attire for every occasion. Of course, owning your own full-length fur coat has definite advantages. Coordinating the perfect accessories, especially collars, adds the final touch. Therefore, the well-groomed cat never appears out of place.

Cats are Xenophobic

• • ❖ • •

Cats are excitable creatures and are frightened by other animals, especially large dogs. Humans who insist upon introducing a dog to a feline-dominated household would be wise to select a pooch with the right disposition. Cats prefer dogs who are unimposing or passive by nature.

Cats are Younghearted

Cats have always known the secrets of youth and vitality. First: no work, all play. Second: relax, the grass on the other side is never greener. Why search for the fountain of youth when you have a birdbath in your own backyard?

Cats are Zany

••❖••

There's no such thing as an ordinary housecat.
Expect the unexpected.

Over the years my cats have revealed to me their secret language in return for my undying devotion. Cats are brilliant conversationalists. Many of the paintings for this book were actually my cats' ideas.

A special note to those who have acquired this book: my cats wish you to know that their gratitude will bring you good fortune, since you will be forever revered by all of catkind.